The Story of

KNOODLE WORLD™

with KURLEY

A MOVIE MUSICAL SCRIPT

and the KLovable Knoodlebugs

By Jean Andersen Harter

iUniverse®

THE STORY OF KURLEY AND THE KNOODLEBUGS
A MOVIE MUSICAL SCRIPT

iUniverse books may be ordered through booksellers or by contacting:

iUniverse
1663 Liberty Drive
Bloomington, IN 47403
www.iuniverse.com
1-800-Authors (1-800-288-4677)

Because of the dynamic nature of the Internet, any web addresses or links contained in this book may have changed since publication and may no longer be valid. The views expressed in this work are solely those of the author and do not necessarily reflect the views of the publisher, and the publisher hereby disclaims any responsibility for them.

Any people depicted in stock imagery provided by Thinkstock are models, and such images are being used for illustrative purposes only.
Certain stock imagery © Thinkstock.

ISBN: 978-1-4917-4711-7 (sc)
ISBN: 978-1-4917-4712-4 (e)

Printed in the United States of America.

iUniverse rev. date: 12/23/2014

Visit Kurley's website at wwwkurley'sknoodleworld.com

A MOVIE MUSICAL

SCRIPT

*   *   *

TITLE: KURLEY and The KLOVABLE

KNOODLEBUGS

AUTHOR: Jean Andersen Harter

SCRIPT: 120 pages

MUSIC: 14 Original songs and skits

SONGWRITERS: Jean Andersen Harter and

KEVIN ANDERSON

MUSIC: Jean has written the story and words to music

*   *   *

KEVIN has composed and arranged and performed the songs.
KEVIN put the words to music.

CAST OF CHARACTERS

1. KURLEY KNOODLE, leader of the world

2. Seven or more KNOODLEBUGS

3. GREAT GRANDFATHER KNU

4. KUDDLES KNUDDLE (love interest of KURLEY

5. The EVIL EKON from the planet EKON

6. TRINIDAD (the faithful dog)

7. MITTON the KNOODLE KITTEN

8. MS HONEYBEE, teacher of KNOODLE WORLD

SONGS in STORY

1. Welcome To KNOODLE WORLD

2. THE EVIL EKON SONG

3. HO! HO! A merry OH!!

4. It MUST HAVE BEEN A GIRLY, GIRL.

5. SOMEWHERE IN A DREAM

6. BEFORE YOU SAY GOODBYE (a waltz)

7. It's A GREAT BIG KLOVABLE DAY

8. ONE little, TWO little KNOODLEBUGS

9. The SUNDAY – MONDAY SONG

10. ThE KLOVEBUG SONG

11. The RAINBOW WISHING RING SONG

12. SOMEWHERE IN A DREAM
    (Now the day has finally come)

13. GRAND FINALE SONG . . . . .

14. KURLEY'S RECIPE FOR A "GREAT BIG KLOVABLE WORLD"

KNOODLE WORLD INTRODUCTION

*   *   *

YOU are about to meet and read about some of MOST exciting and important cartoon characters of the

21st Century . . . . .

"The KLOVABLE

KNOODLEBUGS"

KIND, COURAGEOUS, CONFIDENT,

CLEAN, COOL AND COMPASSIONATE.

(helping to build a KIND world)

Now there are lots of good "bugs" in this world like LADY BUGS, JUNE BUGS Lightning Bugs, Love Bugs and at Disneyland there is even a "BUGS WORLD".

So now we have the "KLOVABLE KNOODLEBUGS" . . . . . plus a new bug, The KLOVE BUG" . . . . .

So enjoy our story 'cause" It's A GREAT BIG KLOVABLE WORLD" with Kurley and KLOVABLE KNOODLEBUGS.

PART ONE

*   *   *

OUR STORY is about KURLEY and KLovable Knoodlebugs . . . . . Great Grandfather KNU . . . the Evil Ekon and how kindness and compassion can change a man's heart.

Jean Andersen Harter

The Wonderful World of KNU
PRELUDE

*   *   *

There was a land that I once knew

A wondrous land known as KNU

Where Great Grandfather did reside

And I would sit there by his side

And hear his tales of love and peace

I hope these days would never cease

But bye and bye he called me in

And said a "new world should begin

Reminding me that

Knowledge is king

And I must learn

Of everything

*   *   *

Now let me take you by the hand

We'll travel to this distant land

Beyond the stars – Beyond the hill

We'll find this land – I know we will

*   *   *

We may pass Mars – and Saturn too and waiting there for me
and you a wondrous land where we may be where people live
in harmony

*   *   * Kurley "K"

SO . . . . . .

WELCOME TO KNOODLE WORLD

and

SOUND the TRUMPETS and

SOUND the BELLS

The KNOODLES are coming to town . . . . . They're coming from here . . . . . They're coming from there . . . . . They're coming from all around

*   *   *

So WELCOME to KNOODLE WORLD and to the KNOODLEBUGS . . . . .

Where KINDNESS and COMPASSION are where everybody is a STAR

Where COURAGE and CONFIDENCE Abound . . . . . where the wonderful world of KNU is found.

So Welcome to KNOODLE WORLD and to Kurley and to the KLOVABLE KNOODLEBUGS.

ONCE UPON A TIME

Long, long ago there was a place called

KNOODLE WORLD where Kurley and the KLOVABLE KNOODLEBUGS lived.

They were so happy there. There was KIND KnoodleBug, Courageous KnoodleBug, Confident, Clean, Kool and compassionate KnoodleBug.

They all loved to go to KURLEY'S Kitchen where they feasted on Knoodle Soup and Knoodle Pizza, a favorite of all KNOODLEBUGS.

They also liked to go to a big castle where GREAT GRANDFATHER KNU lived. He was a great man and they loved to go and hear his stories told from his WORLD BOOKS of KNOWLEDGE and WISDOM on:

How to be KIND

How to be Courageous

How to be Confident

How to be Clean

How to be COOL

How to be Compassionate

They would sit there by his big fireplace in his chambers and listen and learn and laugh and cry and how the time would just fly by.

They would hear his stories of love and peace and hope these days would never cease.

But bye and bye they did go home and Great Grandfather KNU was all alone.

Then one day while Great Grandfather KNU was sound asleep . . . . . someone crept into his chambers deep and alas . . . They stole his World Books of KNOWLEDGE on How to be KIND, courageous, confident, clean, cool and compassionate.

OH my, oh my, exclaimed Great Grandfather KNU, what shall I do . . . . . did this intruder leave a clue? Who would do this horrific thing! To him only sadness and sorrow will bring.

PLANET-EKON

Then upon his fireplace high there was a note Oh my! Oh my!

He read the note and it did say:

"The EVIL EKON was here today".

And stole your books of wisdom and knowledge away. "Now your kingdom will surely fall . . . . .'cause you won't have any wisdom at all.

The EVIL EKON

From The Planet Ekon

EKON", he shouted aloud, "why this can't be. He used to be a friend to me"!

This calls for action right away, I'll call KURLEY and the KNOODLEBUGS with no delay. We'll have a meeting in my chambers today.

When Kurley and the BUGS heard about this terrible dilemma they quickly gathered together for a trip to KNU KINGDOM and to help Great Grandfather KNU.

They arrived at this Castle door and entered into a huge room with a large long table . . . . . reserved for kings and queens for dining and discussions.

Entered Great Grandfather KNU . . . . . "What shall we do"? he asked. Our books of Wisdom and Knowledge have been stolen. This man used to be our friend. He was a king you know . . . . . a king with everything. AND NOW he has deceived me and himself with an act of dishonesty.

Kurley and the BUGS all looked at each other and felt very sad for Great Grandfather KNU

THEN Great Grandfather arose from his big red velvet chair and said "I need three volunteers to journey up to THE PLANET EKON and see what conditions the planet is in. You may also pay a visit to the EVIL EKON.

Kurley and Courageous and Confident KnoodleBug all arose for the occasion.

PLANET

EKON

KURLEY . . . . . COURAGEOUS

AND CONFIDENT

VISIT THE PLANET EKON

They would journey up to the PLANET EKON and visit the EVIL EKON.

It was a long tedious trip but, they were equipped for anything they might find. When they arrived at the Planet EKON they were dismayed and horrified.

The PLANET EKON was in shambles. The trees were whithered and dead and fallen to the ground . . . . . there was no green grass nor flowers to be found. The brooks and streams and rivers were dry as they could be . . . . . and ner' a bird nor sparrow was singing from a tree.

There was not a squirrel nor rabbit gathering its fare. Only a frog and opossum crocking in despair.

There was not a rooster crowing nor a fish swimming in a pond. All these "gifts of nature" from PLANET EKON have been long gone.

It was a sad day for Kurley and the KNOODLEBUGS but now they must be strong for now they must encounter a man who calls himself . . . . . the great and EVIL EKON.

*   *   *

Then they pierced through the palace windows that were shattered . . . . . 2x2 and knocked on the palace door but to no avail . . . . And through the window they saw the EVIL EKON appearing pale and weak and frail. And lying by his bedside was the only friend he had, a dog named TRINIDAD who was always dressed in PLAID. But the scene through the palace window was sad, sad, sad, sad, sad.

They had seen enough and now they would return to KNU KINGDOM and report to Great Grandfather KNU.

The KNOODLEBUGS were anxiously awaiting there. They assembled again at Great Grandfather's table.

Kurley stood –up and he did proclaim "the news it is not good!
The PLANET is in shambles and it is such a shameful shame!
No trees, no grass, no fish, no water, no birds,. no animals,
no flowers to behold. The palace walls are crumbling and the
doors are withering and old.

But worst of all a man, once king, who now had lost his pride
and now his only faithful friend, a dog, who sits there by his
side.

*   *   * As KURLEY said these words a big tear rolled down
the cheek of Great Grandfather KNU. He felt for his friend
EKON and though he had deceived him he wanted to retrieve
him . . . . . his honesty and pride.

Then KNU gathered his thoughts – what to do, what to do? I'll ask each of the KNOODLEBUGS what to do!

The first BUG he called on was KIND KNOODLEBUG. "KIND what would you do?" KIND BUG responded,

I'd show some kindness that's the thing to do

Don't you think showing

Kindness is the thing to do?

Just then CLEAN KNOODLEBUG spoke up.

"As CLEAN BUG I think we should go and CLEAN – UP his PLANET! CLEAN it from top to bottom, to side to side, round to round till not a spot of dirt is found".

Plant new flowers, plant new trees, bring in animals from A to Z's Fill rivers and brooks with water blue and fill them with frogs and fishes too.

Paint palace walls a sparkling white so they glow and shine at night . . . . . trimmed in gold and burgundy . . . . a welcome sight for all to see.

*   *   * All the KNOODLEBUGS were excited. They danced and danced around the Castle floor . . . . . then they danced and danced some more.

They really liked CLEAN'S idea too. Clean – up the planet was the thing to do!

ALAS it was time for CONFIDENT KNOODLEBUG to have his say, "I'm confident this is the right way, I'm ready to start to work today!

Then COOL and COURAGEOUS spoke – up too, "WE think this is the coolest thing to do".

COOL KNOODLEBUG

Kindness and compassion will always be in fashion and it never hurts to always keep your cool . . . . .

COOL BUG

COURAGEOUS KNOODLEBUG

Use courage and compassion and plenty of common – sense . . . . . It never takes much courage to be kind . . . . .

COURAGEOUS BUG

Then COMPASSIONATE KNOODLEBUG was heard to say "we need to show compassion today".

The new best thing that we could do is make him a KNOODLE soup or STEW.

YEAH! They are yelled that's what we'll do . . . We'll make him a KNOODLE stew

They danced and danced on

The castle floor then they danced and danced some more

Then they sang this song.

*   *   *

He is the Evil Ekon he thinks he is so smart.

He has a wicked mind and he has an evil heart.

But EKON, EKON will get you in the end, will try to change your evil heart to good and make you to a friend . . . . . .

And if at first we don't succeed we'll try and try again. The KLovable Knoodlebugss

Great Grandfather KNU was very pleased with what they planned to do . . . . . showing kindness and compassion was the best thing they could do.

PART TWO

RETURN TO PLANET EKON

*   *   *

KURLEY and ALL the KNOODLEBUGS

RETURN TO PLANET EKON

TO RESTORE and CLEAN THE PLANET

Part two

*   *   *

THE KNOODLEBUGS

GO TO WORK

*   *   *

HO! HO! HO! It is off to work we go! With chutes and ladders and hammers and nails and lot and lots of paint and pails.

Buckets of water for river and creeks and the islands too – so they may reflect a beautiful rainbow in a sky of blue.

Bring in animals of every kind, plant trees that sway in the breeze.

Then don't forget the honeybees and birds for singing in the trees . . . . . and bring along a "hankerchief" in case you need to sneeze. And to do all this and to plant each FLOWER . . . . . it's going to take KNOODLE POWER . . . . YEAH!

They loaded the jeeps and trucks and planes . . . . . jet propelled with jet propane.

They would work all day from dawn to dusk then started all over again . . . . . until their work was finally done . . . . . and then they said "AMEN"

UPON their arrival at PLANET EKON . . . . . COMPASSIONATE KNOODLEBUG had a task to do . . . . . He had to leave the EVIL EKON some KNOODLE STEW.

He crept up to the palace door and left a package on the floor. There was a note and it did say,

"YOU'VE HAD A VISITOR TODAY"

Dear Ekon,

We hope you are feeling better. We left you 7 bowls for 7 days and on the 7th day you should feel like NEW with our KNOODLE STEW.

BEST WISHES,

The KLOVABLE KNOODLEBUGS

And COMPASSIONATE BUG also left a little kitten whose name from "mitten". And everyone was smitten with the KNOODLE KITTEN whose name was MITTEN . . . . . MEOW.

He left the kitten with a big pink bow on top of the box with the KNOODLE STEW.

Compassionate Bug returned to work with all the other Bugs.

Ekon and his dog Trinidad were lying on his bed when they heard MEOW . . . . . MEOW . . . . . MEOW . . . . . "what is that sound, Trinidad? Let's go see! Ekon was very weak and frail and pale but, he and Trinidad crawled across the palace floor and opened up the palace door. Then Lo and behold to their surprise was a KNOODLE KITTEN with big blue eyes.

My name is MITTEN

The KNOODLE KITTEN

Everyone is smitten

By this KNOODLE KITTEN

MEOW

The next note said

I'm a lonely little kitten whose

  Name is MITTEN and I really

  Need a place to call my home.

   Won't you take me in and

  Let the love begin . . . so I won't

  Feel afraid and all alone

    MITTEN

    KITTEN

 The Evil Ekon's heart was melting bye and bye. Even TRINIDAD was smitten by the Kitten they called MITTEN . . . . . and soon they would be . . . . a "happy family"! Oh my! Oh my!

MY NAME

Is

TRINIDAD

And I'm always dressed in plaid. The EVIL EKON is my master and he's really not that bad! He feeds me every day and I try to keep his tears away.

He is a lonely, lonely man and I try to cheer him when I can.

TRINIDAD

PLANET-EKON

So EKON, TRINIDAD and Mitten the KNOODLE Kitten all sat down at a big round table in the kitchen and began feasting on KNOODLE STEW.

"Who are these BUGS anyway? . . . . . The KNOODLEBUGS? Are they related to the JUNE Bugs, the Lightning bugs or Love bugs? . . . . any way they seem like GOOD BUGS!!

So for 7 days from 7 bowls they ate and ate KNOODLE STEW . . . . . and everyday EKON became stronger and stronger then on the 7th day he arose from his bed and said "I feel as strong as a BEAR . . . . . maybe a KNOODLE BEAR.

"TRINIDAD, he said BE PREPARED; We're going to walk the planet today and see what we can do to make it look like new"!

He put on his cloak and dagger and hat and walked towards the door with TRINIDAD and MITTEN close behind.

Now what he was about to see would fill his heart with extacsy . . . . He'd smiled and laughed and danced with glee . . . . . the planet filled with greenery . . . . . trees and flowers growing high a beauty he could not deny.

He skipped from tree to tree, brook to brook, creek to creek and drank from a river nearby. He watched a sparrow, a seagull and eagle flying high in the sky. Birds were singing, bells were ringing, his tears he could not hide . . . . . as TRINIDAD and MITTEN were close there by his side.

His heart was filled with so much joy . . . . . his tears he could not hide.

He skipped from tree to tree

and drank from a river nearby

His tears he could not hide

with TRINIDAD and MITTEN

close there by his side

The PLANET EKON

was

RESTORED

[[planet image]]

the BIRDS DID SING the FISH DID SWIM

there was joy in

the Planet once

again

THE PLANET EKON
WAS RESTORED

"Behold, he said and Alas! — Whatever animal, man or beast has done this great thing for me . . . . . I will reward him OPENLY . . . . . I'll give him diamonds, rubies, pearls and treasures beyond belief . . . . . in hopes that he'll forgive me . . . . . as once I was a thief".

I didn't steal his jewels nor lore for this I have been stacking . . . . . I only wanted his wisdom and knowledge —— for this I am sorely lacking.

WITH THIS he found an old oak tree of which an owl did rest. He looked at the owl and said:

"Wise OWL I'm going to try my best . . . . . to change my evil ways and become a man of dignity and honor . . . . . To this I do attest".

Then beneath the old oak tree he removed his cloak, his dagger and hat upon his head . . . . and buried them deep beneath the tree and this is what he said:

"I am no longer the EVIL EKON . . . . . the EVIL EKON, he is dead . . . . . never to rise again and rear his ugly head.

From this day forward I will show kindness to everyone I know.

And kindness and compassion I will always show".

*   *   *

TRINIDAD, EKON and MITTEN the kitten returned to the palace and they were as happy as they could be . . . . . They ate some ginger cookies and sipped on cinnamon tea.

NIGHTTIME CAME and EKON dreamed that someday that he'd have many a friend and that dignity and honor would be bestowed on him again.

The KNOODLEBUGS had been hiding behind the sycamore trees and they were so elated. They had watched while he had removed his gear and buried it beneath the tree where it could never be found . . . . . . beneath the deep, deep ground.

They danced around the old oak tree and then they sang a song:

Ho! Ho! A MERRY OH!

The EVIL KING IS GONE

He won't be back for a million years the evil king is gone!

He took his cloak and dagger and scarf from off his head and buried them beneath a tree and now the evil king is dead.

Ho! Ho! a merry Oh! the evil King is gone. He won't be back for a million years . . . . . the Evil King is dead and gone. He had a change of heart and he changed from bad to good . . . . . now we'll call him the "good EKON" because he is so good".

PART THREE

*   *   *

RETURN TO KNU KINGDOM

And GREAT GRANDFATHER KNU

*   *   *

NOW it was time FOR Kurley and the KNOODLEBUGS to return to KNU KINGDOM and to report to GREAT GRANDFATHER KNU.

They loaded the jeeps, train and aero-plane filled with lots of jet – propane.

AND traveled past an ocean blue, a job fulfilled, a planet cleaned, a planet new.

*   *   *

GREAT GRANDFATHER KNU was joyous over the news that EKON was now a changed man. His heart was changed from EVIL to GOOD as well it should.

AND knowing that the planet was now shiney and new this called for a CELEBRATION or two.

HE hugged the KNOODLEBUGS one by one and said, "a great job has been done"!

"THIS CALLS FOR A CELEBRATION! he exclaimed. A celebration for every nation.

We'll HAVE THEM COME FROM NEAR and FAR

*   *   *

KINGS and QUEENS and MAGITRATES, PRIESTS and Paupers AND POTENTATES . . . . . Rulers and Rulers and HEADS of STATES.

We will invite them ONE and ALL. We're going to have A CHRISTMAS BALL!!

Yeah! They shouted one and all – we're going to have a CHRISTMAS BALL . . . . . they danced around the castle floor and danced and danced and danced some more.

THE KNOODLEBUGS were as excited as they could be . . . . .
dancing in circles 3 x 3. OH what a celebration this will be!
BUT wait . . . . . we haven't seen KURLEY! Where can he be!
We haven't seen him since the clock struck three!

Then COOL KNOODLEBUG spoke up. "I'll go see. I think
he's in the kitchen drinking sassafras tea.

*   *   *

NOW THE LOVE BEGINS . . . . . let the GAMES BEGIN . . . . .

COOL walks into the kitchen and there is KURLEY . . . . .
looking sad and alone and forlorn.

He sits down next to Kurley around the kitchen table. "What's
wrong, KURLEY? You look so sad and forlorn!

Kurley: "Well COOL it's about a GIRL, ... a girly girly
            girl and I can't get her out of my mind!!

CooL: I knew it! It's always about a girl, a girly, girly girl. Now where did you meet this girl?

Kurley: I met her at a ball

Cool: What kind of ball was it?

Kurley: I think it was a Summer Ball, a Fall ball, an Easter Ball, or maybe a Metal ball.

Cool: With all this confusion are you sure it wasn't just an OPTICAL ILLUSION?

Kurley: No! I met her at a ball!

Cool: Well, Kurley, I know about affairs of the heart. I've been there, done that, and maybe I can give you some advice

*   *   *

You cannot sleep, you cannot think, she could be driving you to drink.

Don't you see, you're drowning yourself in Sassafras tea!!

*   *   *

Kurley: Well, I went to my podiatrist

Who said I needed to see a psychiatrist

Who said to see a pharmacist

Who said to see a psychologist

"cause I wasn't sleeping well at night".

*   *   *

They said I maybe need a preventative or maybe a good laxative . . . . . OH! My!

Cool: I do have one little question

Is she causing you indigestion?

Do you find you can't sleep or feel your feet at night?

NOW YOUR MIND IS ALL A MUDDLE

'Cause you found someone you want to CUDDLE.

But I'll tell you what your problem really is!

*   *   *

On the next page is the SONG that KNOODLE BUG sings to KURLEY

SONG
"IT MUST HAVE BEEN A GIRLY, GIRL"!

*   *   *

COOL BUG sings this song to KURLEY . . . . .

*   *   *

It must have been a girly girl, a whirly girl, a squirrely girl whose messing up your mind!

Hair of blonde or brown or red for sure her head is full of lead.

Purple, pink or maybe green . . . . . The craziest hair you've ever seen.

She might be fat

She might be thin

With curves like SOPHIA

OR MAR – I—LYN

*   *   *

A Bathing beauty with

A TAN —

You better go catch her

While you can

She might be living in

A van

A Bathing beauty with

A tan . . . . . OH MAN!

You cannot sleep

You cannot think

She could be driving

You to the brink

*   *   *

It must have been a girly, girl, a whirly girl, a squirrely girl whose messing with your mind.

*   *   *

But Kurley I don't think

You're going to make it on

Your own

*   *   *

You need someone to hold

You tight

You need someone to kiss good night

You need someone to hug and squeeze

Someone to bless you when you sneeze

Now you've got to play

It Cool

Don't tell her that you've been a fool

*   *   *

Tell her she is the one you love

The one that you've been thinking of

*   *   *

She is so cute

She is so sweet

She could make

Your life complete

*   *   *

So catch the next train

Or aero – plane and get

Her on the TELEPHONE and make this girly, whirley, squirrely, girly all your own

*   *   *

Then you'll have some girly

Whirly, squirrely Kids

To call your own

*   *   *

She might be a beauty with a tan

With curves like SOPHIA or

MAR – I – LYN

You better catch her while you can

Get her on the telephone and make this girly, whirley, squirrely, girly ALL your own

The End

The song is over and the mood changes.

KURLEY: You're probably right COOL BUG. Her name is KUDDLES . . . . . but I can't find her. I've searched high and low *   *   *and traveled sea to sea

She is in my dreams and in my memory and KURLEY now sings this beautiful love song called:

SOME WHERE IN A MEMORY"

Words and music by

Andersen and Anderson

*   *   *

SOMEWHERE IN A DREAM and

SOMEWHERE IN A DREAM

*   *   *

There's a you and there's a me.

Somewhere in my memory

Love was yours and love was mine

We said we'd never part

Then you said goodbye to me

AND stole away my heart

*   *   *

And NOW I'd search the whole

WIDE WORLD . . . . . or travel sea to sea

To find the love that's meant for me

FOR TIME and ALL ETERNITY

'Till then I'll find you

Somewhere in a DREAM and

SOMEWHERE in a memory

The End

AS COOL BUG listened a big tear rolled down his face . . . . . he knew how KURLEY felt . . . . . he gave a big Bear hug to KURLEY and then he said, "Hey KURLEY! We are going to have a Ball . . . . . A Christmas Ball right here"!

Kurley: "OH NO! NOT another Ball," he said

Cool: "Yeah, but Kurley you never know who will be there They are coming from near and far and if it's meant to be it's meant to be".

Kurley: You are probably right Cool. I have to keep searching for her.

Because before she said goodbye to me she sang this song to me and it was called . . . . .

"BEFORE WE SAY GOODBYE'

*   *   *

SONG

*   *   *

Whisper to me that you love me

Before you say goodbye

Whisper to me that you'll miss me

Before you say goodbye

Then I will always remember

The days of you and I

When you held me and kissed me

And told me you'd miss me

BEFORE WE SAID GOODBYE

Kuddles Knuddle

This was just too much for COOL BUG. The tears did fall. . . and of course he was suppose to be the coolest BUG of ALL.

*　　*　　*

You must find her KURLEY! You must travel sea to sea . . . . . travel endlessly! 'till then you'll find her only in a dream only and in a memory . . . . .

*　　*　　*

Cool sings: You must remember this

A kiss is still a kiss

A sigh is still a sigh

The ordinary things apply

As time goes by

*　　*　　*

It's STILL the same old story

A fight for love and glory

A case of Do or Die

*   *   *

The world will always

Welcome lovers

AS TIME GOES BY

Song from movie

Casablanca

Cool and Kurley wiped away their tears, stood tall and were ready to meet the world!

Kurley and Cool Knoodlebug left the kitchen and went to the big ballroom where all the KNOODLEBUGS were dancing and singing and getting out lights and decorations, big bows and trees and wreaths for a celebration.

Kurley and KIND and Confident started working on an invitation for the celebration. There was much anticipation in the air. And nothing could compare with the love that was in the air . . . . and they were happy one and all 'cause there was going to be a BALL . . . . . A CHRISTMAS BALL for one and all.

SPECIAL INVITATIONS

Would be sent to everyone and especially to EKON, TRINIDAD and MITTEN, the Knoodle Kitten . . . . . as they would be honored as special guests at the Ball.

*   *   *

Also an invitation would be sent to MS HONEYBEE who is the KNOODLEBUGS school teacher at MS HONEYBEE'S SCHOOL HOUSE.

She could sing and dance and taught the Knoodlebugs many new dances and songs with the KNOODLEBUGS for the Christmas Ball.

Wait til you meet Ms. Honeybee.

She's as pretty as she can be.

Full of sugar and full of spice.

Oh so pretty and oh so nice.

And she's as smart as she can be

Wait til you meet Ms. Honeybee

KNU KINGDOM

YOU ARE CORDIALLY INVITED to attend a CHRISTMAS BALL at KNU KINGDOM

Date: December 15

TIME: 6 oo'clock

Dress: Formal

Dinner and refreshment will be served

Music, Dancing and live Entertainment

HOST: GREAT GRANDFATHER KNU

KURLEY and the Klovable Knoodlebugs

RSVP Thank You

WHEN EKON received the invitation by special delivery he was excited as he could be.

He called in TRINIDAD and MITTEN and said "We're going to be dining with ROYALTY . . . . . We're going to be dressed in FINERY . . . . . BOOTS will be shined to SHINERY . . . . . curls will be curled to CURLERY . . . . . Tails will be FLUFFED to FLUFFERY.

We're going to the BALL!

As for TRINIDAD (who is always dressed in PLAID) we'll design a new plaid suit, the PLAIDEST suit he'd ever had.

AND for MITTEN we'll make her new mittons and bows. We'll find her some polish, some pretty pink polish to polish her pretty pink toes.

*   *   *

We'll arrive there in style and people will smile as we look all shiny and new . . . . . dressed in our finery, shined in our shinery, curled in our curlery, fluffed in our fluffery AND we'll smile back at them too!

Bells will be ringing and people are singing when we arrive at the hall.

Each BUG they will greet us . . . . . they'll hug and they'll squeeze us as we have arrived for the Ball.

THE ONE and ONLY CHRISTMAS BALL!!

*   *   *

BUT they'ed have to wait it was still ten days 'til they could go to the ball.

The KNOODLEBUGS were all so jolly . . . . . decking the halls
with Balls of HOLLY. Fa – ala – ala – ala –la la la

Eating CHOCOLATE, CHEESE and delecacies while trimming
all the Christmas trees.

They'll put a "star" atop each tree . . . . . shining brightly for
all to see. They were as happy as could be – Trimming up each
Christmas tree.

*   *   *

THE KNOODLEBUGS they went shopping . . . . . bought pop
corn for popping, Marshmallows to roast on a fire.

They all bought a "TUXEDO" so they could look "NEATO" and be dressed in the finest attire.

NOW as for KURLEY he's going to look "girly" dressed – up in velvet and lace. With the fur he is carrying and high heels he's wearing WE HOPE HE WON'T FALL ON HIS FACE!!

But we guess he'll look girly — a little bit whirley —'cause he's MASTER of CER-E-MON-Y

The DAY of the BALL
December 15,
THE BIG ARRIVAL

*   *   *

Bells they were ringing

Choristers singing

HARPS they were harping

Trumpeters trumping

The KNOODLEBUGS were dressed to the tee . . . . . as they stood by the big castle door next to the big Christmas tree.

*   *   *

And just for the pleasin' there might be huggin' and squeezin' . . . . . as guests arrive at the door.

THEY were coming from far and from near . . . . . dressed—up in holiday gear.

ARRIVING on stallions and ganders and goose, peacocks and reindeer or was it a moose?

ANIMALS arriving 2 x 2 Elephants, Tigers and a Kangaroo. You'd think that you were at the ZOO. Animals arriving 2 x 2 . . . . .

ARE THERE ANY ANIMALS LEFT at the ZOO??

Then came a caravan of horses and carriages . . . . . Trains and planes and automobiles . . . . . Limosines trimmed with tinsel and frills.

THE guests all gathered in the hall . . . . . awaiting the biggest event of all . . . . . When KING EKON would arrive . . . with Trinidad and MITTEN by his side.

THE CASTLE DOORS opened – they opened wide and throngs of people were waiting inside when a horse – drawn carriage shaped like a CRYSTAL BALL . . . . . with lions and tigers and llames and a giraffe that stood 10 feet tall.

*   *   *

And leading the parade was a great camel bejeweled with diamonds, rubies and pearls. And on his back was a sight to behold.

THE BOOKS of KNOWLEDGE and WISDOM were in a golden box trimmed in diamonds, silver and gold. Sapphires blue, turquoise, too, emerald sparkling green.

It was the most beautiful sight in all the world that they had ever seen.

KING EKON emerged from the carriage, stood tall and he did proclaim – "the WISDOM and KNOWLEDGE contained in these books on HOW TO BE KIND, COURAGEOUS, CONFIDENT, CLEAN, COMPASSIONATE and COOL (things you don't always learn about in school) are worth more than all the jewels, diamonds, silver and gold, sapphires and rubies too . . . . . and today I am returning them to GREAT GRANDFATHER KNU.

The crowd cheered and cried in excitement . . . . . They stood and clapped aloud as KNU and EKON embraced each other so happy and so proud.

The trumpets blew, the orchestra played as Trinidad and MITTEN emerged from the CRYSTAL BALL . . . . . Smiling proudly, cheering loudly, lighting up the CHRISTMAS HALL.

THEN Kurley who was dressed kind of girly in his suit of VELVET and LACE . . . . .

He greeted each guest and bowed to each one and hoped he wouldn't fall on HIS FACE.

*   *   *

THE CORONATION
of
EKON
As he is crowned
The GOOD KING EKON

THE CORONATION

*   *   *

Now KNU and all the KLOVABLE BUGS were seated on the stage in big RED VELVET CHAIRS.

King EKON and KNU walked to the center stage.

KNU spoke: "KING EKON, you will be CROWNED . . . . . a new title, a new name that will last you for many an age.

*   *   *

I hereby proclaim:

From this day forward

From this day on

You will be addressed

And known as

"THE GOOD KING EKON"

Church bells did RING – the choirs did SING the guests they cheered as never before.

The BUGS they did dance

Great grandfather danced

And KURLEY danced and

He fell on his face on the floor!!

*   *   *

The crowd broke – out in laughter from this dancing disaster but, Kurley stood tall and said, "I'll be FINE"!! He arose with great style and with a big smile and announced:

"WE ARE READY TO DINE"!

*   *   *

A SPECIAL, SPECIAL SURPRISE was in store for everyone. A new culinary dish would be served for all . . . . . at the ball.

They would be feasting on KNOODLE SOUP, KNOODLE STEW and KNOODLE PIZZA. And a new item would be added to the menu that was TOP SECRET.

A DRUM ROLL PLEASE

*   *   *

Waiters were coming out of the kitchen carrying platters and platters of KNOODLE FRIED CHICKEN . . . . .

Good for the Licken

KNOODLE

FRIED

CHICKEN

*   *   *

The crowd was all a buzzin' and happy as they devoured the new KNOODLE FRIED CHICKEN . . . . . good for the licken.

AFTER DINING came the dancing and a night of GREAT ENTERTAINMENT.

*　　*　　*

Kurley was the Master of Ceremony (the Emcee). The BUGS would be billed as THE SINGING and DANCING KNOODLEBUGS with guest star Ms. HONEYBEE.

*　　*　　*

An elegant program was given each guest listing each song and skit and dance to be performed.

Kurley as

"Master of Ceremony"

at GRAND Christmas Ball

KNU KINGDOM

PROGRAM

of

ENTERTAINMENT

December 15th

1. POEM by Courageous KNOODLEBUG
   It's A GREAT BIG KLOVABLE Day by Confident
   KNOODLEBUG

2. Ms HONEYBEE and BUGS sing a special song

3. Ms. Honeybee and BUGS sing THE "SUNDAY/
   MONDAY" SONG

4. The KLOVEBUG Song sung by Kurley

5. "Now the Day has Finally come" sung by Kurley

6. The GRAND FINALE SONG

7. Kurley "Recipe for a KLOVABLE WORLD

8. "The Rainbow Wishing Ring Song" sung by the
   Knoodlebugs

Excitement mounted as the orchestra started playing, the stage curtain was drawn and KURLEY walked triumphantly to the microphone.

LADIES and GENTLEMAN, ANIMALS, Ants, BEES and FLEAS. Welcome to a night of ENTERTAINMENT!!

*   *   *

The first KNOODLEBUG to entertain you is COURAGEOUS BUG with a poem.

COURAGEOUS KNOODLEBUG appears on stage and takes the microphone.

*   *   *

'TWAS the night before Christmas and all through the garage

THE TIRES were hung on the rafters with CARE

In hopes that Santa soon would be there to fill up the tires with air.

*   *   *

Laughter, laughter came from the crowd as COURAGEOUS continued the poem

*   *   *

He fell from the rooftop and he fell from the rafters

But then I heard Santa say:

"Don't worry and be of of good cheer

Santa will be back next year

To fill – up your tires

With air"

The crowd roared with laughter as KURLEY said: "Thank you Courageous BUG

*   *   *

KURLEY: Now CONFIDENT BUG
will sing:
It's A GREAT BIG
KLOVABLE DAY'

*   *   *

It's a great big Klovable day, Everythings going to go my way
Not a cloud in the sky Happy people walking by on this great
big Klovable Day Today . . . . .

*   *   *

(Bridge) AND I say to myself I'm going to smile today and I
say to myself I'm going to sing.

*   *   *

   And myself answers back

   In the cleverest way smile and to sing in

   My most unusual way

*   *   *

"Cause it's a great Klovable

World to live in.

Great big Klovable

Even K'Like-able

GREAT BIG KLOVABLE DAY

*   *   *

The end

CLAP, CLAP, CLAP, from the crowd.

KURLEY: Thank you Confident Bug – that's a great way to start the day!

*   *   *

KURLEY: NOW we are proud to INTRODUCED

Ms HONEYBEE from Ms. Honeybee's

SCHOOL HOUSE (where all KNOODLEBUGS attend school)

Ms. HONEYBEE and the KNOODLEBUGS take center stage.
The BUGS line—up and sing.

SONG

And DANCE

*   *   *

One little, two little, three

Knoodle BUGS

Four little, five little, six

KNOODLEBUGS

Seven little, eight little

Nine KNOODLE BUGS

TEN KNOODLEBUGS

*   *   *

OH! Ten little, nine little, eight

KNOODLE BUGS

Seven little, six little, five

KNOODLE BUGS

Four little, three little,

Two little KNOODLE BUGS

ONE KNOODLE BUG

The end

Everyone clapped and clapped.

*   *   *

A SONG and SKIT

Ms. Honeybee is now on stage and writes a letter . . . . .

TO: MR WEBSTER of WEBSTER'S DICTIONARY

FROM: Citizens of Knoodle World and Ms.

Honeybee, school teacher

DEAR MR. WEBSTER:

We citizens of Knoodle World would like to change your dictionary. We hereby proclaim that it is proper in the English language to spell the following words with a "C" or a "K".

COURAGE and CONFIDENCE, COMPASSION and COMMON-SENSE, CO-OPERATION and CONSIDERAION.

KINDNESS and KNOWLEDGE ARE ALWAYS spelled with a "K" . . . . . but the others can be spelled either way . . . . . they can be spelled with a "C" or spelled with a "K" . . . . . as long as they are "used".

Always remember to use KOURAGE and KONFIDENCE and plenty of KOMMON-SENSE. AND KO-OPERATION and KONSIDERATION will make for a better nation.

Thank You,

CITIZENS of KNOODLE WORLD

*   *   *

"Yeah"! yelled the KNOODLEBUGS. We can spell them either way. We can spell them with a "C" or spell them with a "K" and we still will get an "A".

Thank you, Ms. Honeybee that's KURLEY with a "K".

A third song would delight the crowd called:
"THE SUNDAY – MONDAY SONG"

@ J. Andersen Harter

Sung by The Klovable Knoodlebugs

"THE SUNDAY – MONDAY SONG"

*   *   *

OH! I love the Mon in Monday

I love the Tue in Tuesday

I love the Wed in Wednesday

HOW ABOUT YOU

*   *   *

I love the Thur. in Thursday

I love the Fri in Friday

I love the Sat in Saturday

HOW ABOUT YOU

And we love the SUN in SUNDAY AND WE LOVE YOU.

AND we LOVE THE SUN in SUNDAY and we love you

Monday, Tuesday, Wednesday, Thursday, Friday, Saturday and SUNDAY

AND WE LOVE YOU!!!

TheKLOVABLE KNOODLEBUGS

*   *   *

The audience clapped and cheered and repeated:

"WE LOVE the SUN in Sunday and we love you"

*   *   *

COMPASSIONATE BUG comes out and takes the microphone

Compassionate . . . . . . "KURLEY, I understand that you have solved THE MYSTERY of LOVE"!

* * *

KURLEY: YES, I have!

COMPASSIONATE: So . . . . . KURLEY, You'll go down in history if you have solved the mystery of love

THE KLOVEBUG SONG

KURLEY: sings:

Well, I went to my optometrist, then to an oculist, then to an acupuncturist and to a doctor and a dentist too

BUT NONE OF THEM EVEN HAD A CLUE

*   *   *

I ASKED: Is there a vaccination to stop this infatuation . . . . . that causes so much aggregation and no one had a clue of what to do!!

*   *   *

Then as luck would have it

I was standing by a tree and a little birdy found me and helped me solve this

MYSTERY!

He said: It's The KLOVEBUG

Who has found you

The KLOVEBUG did

Surround you

AND you have been bitten by the

KLOVEBUG of LOVE

*   *   *

Your heart is all a flutter

Your knees have turned to butter

AND you wouldn't have it any other way

*   *   *

Love is what makes life worth living

The loving and forgiving the

Pain and all the sorrow that's

Sure to come tomorrow

*   *   *

AND you wouldn't have it any other way

So find yourself someone to

Love you TODAY

*   *   *

The KLOVEBUG will get you from behind

AND then you're going to find that love is everywhere that love is in the air

*   *   *

So go tell your sister and your mother, your father and your brother and all the stars from up above

That everyone for centuries have been smitten and bitten by

THE KLOVEBUG of love!!!

KURLEY!!

The KLOVEBUG will get you if you DON'T WATCH OUT!!

AND that is the mystery of Love!

The end

The crowd clapped and cheered loudly.

*   *   *

Just then KURLEY was called backstage by the BUGS.

*   *   *

COOL BUG came to the center stage and had an announcement to make.

*   *   *

Dear GUESTS . . . . . "we have a SECRET to share with you about KURLEY. ABOUT 2 years ago KURLEY met a girl at a ball. HE FELL IN LOVE . . . . . Her name is KUDDLES and he has not been able to find her. He says he has looked high and low and traveled sea to sea to find her . . . . . and to no avail.

BUT ladies and gentlemen, Animals, ants, bugs, bees and fleas — tonight KUDDLES will be here!! The BUGS and I have found her!!!

When KIURLEY comes out she should appear and KURLEY's heart will fall to the ground — as we have finally found KUDDLES".

*   *   *

The audience was all excited and happy for KURLEY and KUDDLES TOO.

Great anticipation and excitement filled the air

Soon KURLEY appeared on the stage and started to speak when he heard someone softly call "KURLEY ", KURLEY". He turned around and to his GREAT SURPRISE there was KUDDLES standing there right before his eyes!

*   *   *

KUDDLES, he cried, "you've come back to me", He quickly ran to her side embraced her and kissed her and sang this song:

SONG

* * *

NOW THE DAY has finally come

You have returned to me

AND now you're more than

Just a dream

AND just a memory

* * *

Now they'll always be a you

And always be a me . . . . .

WE'LL be together

Together You and ME

FOR TIME and ALL ETERNITY

The end

KURLEY took Kuddles in his arms and kissed her again while the crowd was cheering and crying and smiling. They were so happy to see this beautiful couple in love.

*   *   *

THE GRAND FINALE

*   *   *

Kurley returned to the microphone with KUDDLES by his side.

KURLEY: "Everyone – we want you all on stage for our Grand Finale Song".

GRAND FINALE SONG

By

Andersen and Anderson

*   *   *

AND it's a great big KLOVABLE

WORLD we live in

GREAT BIG KLOVABLE WORLD

There's smiles all around

There's KLOVE to be found

It' a great big KLOVABLE

World all around

*   *   *

AND it's a mother's world and

A father's world

A grandmother, grandfather

Grandchild's world

What a wonderful world

It's a Great Big KLOVABLE

World all around

*   *   *

AND it's a People's World,

Yes A PEOPLE'S World

It's doctor and a lawyer

AND a postman's world

*   *   *

AND it's a SPORTY WORLD

It's an OLYMPIC WORLD . . . . .

It's baseball, football and basketball world

What a wonderful, wonderful world

AND it's a DISNEYLAND WORLD,

It's a MICKEY MOUSE WORLD

It's a KNOTTS BERRY WORLD

It's a SNOOPY WORLD

*   *   *

It's a Col. Sanders World

It's a Ronald Mc Donald World

It's a French fry, Hamburger and

Malted World

*   *   *

It's A SANTA CLAUS WORLD

*   *   *

It's a SANTA CLAUS WORLD?

Just then COURAGEOUS BUG interrupts the song by coming
on stage and recites his poem:

'TWAS THE NIGHT BEFORE CHRISTMAS and there was a knock at the door. It was Mrs SANTA CLAUS standing there as never before!

She said: "Santa will not be back anymore to fill – up your tires with air".

He fell from the ROOFTOP

He fell from the RAFTERS

He fell on the floor

He fell on the stair

He'll NEVER be back to fill your tires with air.

*   *   *

Don't you know that

SANTA IS JUST FULL OF HOT AIR!

*   *   *

The crowd roared with laughter and the song continued . . . . .

*   *   *

Then each KNOODLEBUG comes out and sings

It's a kind, kind world

It's a Courageous World

It's a confident World

It's a clean, clean World

It's a compassionate World

It's a cool, cool World

It's A GREAT BIG KLOVABLE WORLD. ThE BUGS march and sing GLORY, GLORY, HALLELUJAH!

His truth is marching on

*   *   *

And it's a RELIGIOUS WORLD

It's a Muslim, and a Jewish and a

CHRISTIAN WORLD

*   *   *

It's still the same old story . . . . .

A fight for love and glory

A case of DO or DIE

*   *   *

Just then KIND BUG and COMPASSIONATE BUG appear and say:

"Can't We all just get along world" . . . . .

They all sing

It's every body's world

IT'S A great big klovable world to

Live in:

VERY KLOVABLE

EVEN K-LIKE—ABLE

GREAT BIG KLOVABLE WORLD! SOMEWHERE in A DREAM and SOMEWHERE in memory THERE'S A YOU AND THERE'S and me in a great big KLOVABLE WORLD!

The end

It's still the same old story . . .

A fight for love and glory

A case of DO or DIE

and remember

The KLOVEBURG WILL GET YOU IF YOU DON'T WATCH OUT!!

Then Kurley sings this song:
"SONG"

KURLEY'S RECIPE

(pic) for

A GREAT BIG

KLOVABLE WORLD

*   *   *

ONE CUP of KINDNESS

TWO CUPS of CLEAN

THREE CUPS of KLOVE and a little less mean

*   *   *

Stir with COURAGE and CONFIDENCE use plenty of COMMON – SENSE

For a great Big Klovable World

Then take out the AGGRAVATION

Use a little SOPHISTICATION with a ton of DETERMINATION

And NO DISCRIMINATION

*   *   *

For a GREAT BIG Klovable World to

LIVE IN

VERY KLOVABLE . . . . . EVEN K-LIKE-ABLE GREAT BIG KLOVABLE WORLD

The end

Thank you

KURLEY "K"

AFTER KURLEY sings his recipe for a KLOVABLE WORLD . . . . .

Kurley stays on stage to announce the final song.

*   *   *

May I present

THE KNOODLE WORLD

SINGERS and DANCERS singing

THE RAINBOW
WISHING RING SONG

THE RAINBOW WISHING RING SONG

*   *   *

There's a Rainbow Wishing Ring

Shades of red and white and blue

And if you wish upon the rainbow

Your wishes may come true

*   *   *

It's wishing love to everyone from sea to shining sea

OH the colors of the Rainbow

Wishing love to you and me

There's a star to wish upon and there's a magic wand

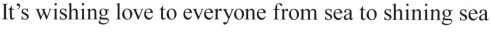

and there is a rainbow in the sky

For you to wish upon

*   *   *

So if you see a rainbow in a sky of blue

If you wish upon the rainbow

Your wishes may come true the end

ThE KLOVABLE KNOODLE BUGS from around the world

HAVE A KLOVABLE DAY

IT'S A GREAT BIG

KLOVABLE WORLD

THE END

THE KLOVEBUG WILL GETCHA
IF YOU DON'T WATCH OUT!!

THANK YOU for reading our story and hope that you have enjoyed it . . . . . and we hope that someday you will see us on the BIG SILVER SCREEN as a MOVIE MUSICAL and or in a BROADWAY MUSICAL.

Lots of Klove,

Kurley and the Knoodlebugs

*   *   *

*A NOTE FROM THE AUTHOR
STAGE PLAY……………...

We encourage this book to be used as a guideline for a stage play to be performed by grade schools, high schools, colleges, and theater groups as a positive learning tool! VISIT Kurley on Facebook. Music is available on iTunes, AMAZON, etc. Go to WWW.KNOODLEWORLDSING-A-LONG.COM
Kurley's website: www.thinkstockphotos.com
E-mail us at dharter7@cox.net

ABOUT the AUTHOR

Jean Andersen Harter, creator of Knoodle World and its characters is President and CEO of the KIND WORLD PROJECT for children. She was educated at UCI, the University of California at IRVINE and BYU, Provo, Utah. She has a degree in elementary education.

Jeans' husband, Derris Harter has a Masters degree in School Administration from USC, the University of Southern California and served as a school principal in Europe for the U.S. military for 35 years.

Together they have 6 children and 13 grandchildren and five in the coastal town of San

Clemente, California. Jean and Derris married in 2011 when she was 78 years and he was 84.

When Derris learned of this exceptional, positive project for children he encouraged Jean to continue writing and she finished the musical in the year 2014. An amazing story with amazing cartoon characters designed to instill (good character) in children.

It is our hope that it will help kids of the world to be KIND, COURAGEOUS, CONFIDENT and COMPASSIONATE etc. so needed in our world today.

Thank You,

Jean Andersen Harter

CAST of CHARACTERS

****

Kurley Knoodle

Leader of Knoodle World

****

****

GREAT GRANDFATHER

"KNU"

The KLOVABLE KNOODLEBUGS

KIND, COURAGEOUS, CONFIDENT,
CLEAN, COOL and COMPASSIONATE

The EVIL EKON

From the Planet Ekon

KURLEY Dressed-up

For EASTER BALL and

Christmas BALL and

MASTER of CEREMONY

KUDDLES KNUDDLE

Love interest of

Kurley Knoodle

MS HONEYBEE

Teacher of the

KNOODLEBUGS

TRINIDAD

Faithful Dog of the

EVIL EKON

MITTEN THE

KNOODLE KITTEN

THE EVIL EKON

as changed to the

"GOOD KING EKON"

THE

KLOVEBUG

GRAND FINALE SONG

Many costumed characters will be dressed-up to depict the many people, places and things that make-up our GREAT BIG KLOVABLE WORLD... such as a doctor, lawyer, postman, basketball, football, baseball player, MICKEY MOUSE, SNOOPY, Muslin, Rabbi, Priest, Santa Clause, Ronald McDonald Col. Sanders, etc. and will appear onstage for THE GRAND FINALE SONG.

the Story of

KURLEY and the

KNOODLEBUGS

****

as told by

KUDDLES
KNUDDLE

***

The story in brief

****

ONCE UPON A TIME

. . . . . the KLOVABLE KNOODLEBUGS lived with GREAT GRANDFATHER KNU in KNU KINGDOM . . . . . Kurley was the leader of the crew – He is a little person (not a Bug) AND HE WAS THEIR LEADER. They all loved to go to KURLEY'S KITCHEN where they feasted on KNOODLE SOUP, KNOODLE STEW and KNOODLE PIZZA.

All was happy in KNU KINGDOM and they loved to hear GRANDFATHER KNU tell stories about being KIND, Courageous, Confident etc. and each BUG was named KIND . . . . . COURAGEOUS . . . . . CONFIDENT . . . . . CLEAN . . . . . COMPASSIONATE . . . . and COOL. They called themselves "THE KLOVABLE KNOODLEBUGS.

ONE DAY . . . . . Great Grandfather came to KURLEY and said "How would you and the KNOODLE CREW like to start your own world? "OUR OWN WORLD, grandfather? How can this be"??

"OH this will be fun and exciting, Kurley . . . . . Just you wait and see!!

So KURLEY went to the KNOODLE BUGS and told them that Great Grandfather said that we can start our own world if we like. What do you think?

These KLOVABLE BUGS all liked the idea and they jumped and shouted with joy to think they could start their own world. And it was called KNOODLE WORLD!!!!! B

The Knoodle crew built houses, cabins and churches galore . . . . schools and parks and many a store. They even built a KURLEY's KITCHEN where they could feast on KNOODLE fixins' and everything that would make – up a little world of their own . . . . made of love and plaster and marbles and stone

KURLEY and the KLOVABLE KNOODLE BUGS were very happy in their new world.

From time to time they would visit GREAT GRANDFATHER KNU at KNU KINGDOM and he would read them stories from his KNU WORLD BOOK OF KNOWLEDGE and WISDOM on HOW to BE KIND, Courageous, Confident, Clean, Compassionate and Cool.

THEN ONE DAY . . . . . KNU called KURLEY and told him that while he was fast asleep an intruder came in and STOLE his BOOKS oF KNOWLEDGE and WISDOM away.

He left a note and it did say C

"THE EVIL EKON was here Today and STOLE your BOOKS of KNOWLEDGE and WISDOM away". HA! H A! HA! Now your kingdom will surely fall" cause you won't have any WISDOM at ALL. HA! HA! HA!

The EVIL EKON from The PLANET EKON

When Kurley and the Knoodle crew heard about this they immediately ran up to see GREAT GRANDFATHER KNU to see what they could do to help.

They met in KNU'S chambers and had a BIG Conference. KNU asked 3 Volunteers to visit the Planet EKON and also to check on the EVIL EKON.

After A Visit to Planet EKON they reported back to KNU that the Planet was in Shambles – No trees, no animals, no birds, no water for fishes in brooks, rivers or creeks and that the EVIL D EKON was a very sad and lonely Man and his only friend was his dog TRINIDAD (who was always dressed in plaid) and he appeared weak and frail and pale.

When KNU heard this his heart was saddened. "EKON used to be a friend of mine you know? He was a king with everything"!

So what do you suppose the KNOODLEBUGS decided to do??

Did they want to show KINDNESS and COMPASSION to this lonely man, who once was a king with everything!

What would they do to try to change his evil heart to good?

What about his planet . . . . . could they make it all brand new?

What happened when COMPASSIONATE Knoodlebug left him a KNOODLE KITTEN and a KNOODLE STEW?

AND What happened to me (KUDDLES) and KURLEY who met last year at a BALL and "fell in love". We lost each other and he has been searching for me . . . . . Will he find me again? E

AND what about Ms Honeybee? She's as PRETTY as SHE CAN BE – WAIT 'til you meet Ms Honeybee!!

AND what about the KLOVEBUG? Has KIURLEY solved the MYSTERY of LOVE??

AND will the EVIL EKON ever return the KNU WORLD BOOKS of KNOWLEDGE and WISDOM to GREAT GRANDFATHER KNU??

What happens when invitations are sent to every nation to a GREAT CHRISTMAS BALL?

Will there be a CORINATION? Will the EVIL EKON attend the BALL?

Will KURLEY and I find each other again at the ball? What surprise will be waiting guests at the BALL? Many, many "happy SURPRISES" await the guest at the GREAT CHRISTMAS BALL.

These are questions that are answered in our 120 page book with words to songs and music . . . . .(14 songs)

In our story called:

"IT'S A GREAT BIG KLOVABLE WORLD" . . . . starring KURLEY and THE KLOVABLE KNOODLE BUGS.

. . . . . which we hope will someday be a MOVIE MUSICAL on the BIG SILVER SCREEN and or a Broadway musical.

Thank You Everyone

KUDDLES KNUDDLE

HAVE A KLOVABLE DAY!!

'Cause IT'S A GREAT BIG KLOVABLE WORLD!!

The End

VISIT Kurley on Facebook

music is on i tunes, Amazon,

etc. at KNOODLE WORLD

Sing – A – Long.com

A SPECIAL NOTE

FROM the AUTHOR

***

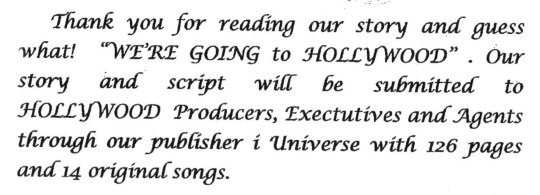

Dear Readers,

Thank you for reading our story and guess what! "WE'RE GOING to HOLLYWOOD". Our story and script will be submitted to HOLLYWOOD Producers, Exectutives and Agents through our publisher i Universe with 126 pages and 14 original songs.

The book is available at BARNES and NOBLE Bookstore and any bookstore in the USA and ordered through publisher i Universe at 1 800 288 4677.

Thank You,

Jean Andersen Harter

Jean Andersen Harter

Email .... dharter7@cox.net

Your comments are welcome and may be forwarded to our publisher.

Have a KLOVABLE Day !

Edwards Brothers Malloy
Oxnard, CA USA
January 15, 2015